DEEPAK CHOPRA

The Wisdom Within

COMPANION BOOK

DEEPAK CHOPRA

The Wisdom Within

COMPANION BOOK

HARMONY BOOKS

NEW YORK

Copyright © 1997 by Crown Publishers, Inc., and Geismar & Groth, Inc.

Published by Harmony Books, a division of Crown Publishers, Inc.,
201 East 50th Street, New York, New York 10022.
Member of the Crown Publishing Group.

Random House, Inc. New York, Toronto, London, Sydney, Auckland

http://www.randomhouse.com/

HARMONY and colophon are trademarks of Crown Publishers, Inc.

Printed in the United States of America

Design by Lynne Amft

ISBN 0-517-88816-5

10   9   8   7   6   5   4   3   2   1

First Edition

CONTENTS

INTRODUCTION

Ayurveda, which means "science of life" in Sanskrit, is the oldest medical system in human history, dating back to roughly 1000 B.C. Yet, remarkably, the guiding principles of this ancient science are continually being proven out today by the latest high-tech research in medicine, physics, and biology. According to Ayurveda, the mind exerts the deepest influence on the body. Freedom from sickness depends upon contacting our own awareness, bringing it into balance, and extending that balance to the body. This state of being, the wellspring of physical immunity, creates a higher state of health.

In *The Wisdom Within*, I provide an introduction to this remarkable ancient system, and to the benefits it can provide for us in the contemporary world. This multimedia program is divided into three sections: Living in Balance, The Field of Infinite Possibilities, and The Sacred Space. It will enable you to discover your unique mind body constitution, which in turn will provide you with a gateway to the essential unity and wholeness that is the true foundation of the universe.

This companion volume to *The Wisdom Within* does not attempt to re-create in print the experience of the program as a whole. Rather, it is intended to serve as a reference for some of the most practical information from the Living in Balance section, which deals specifically with personal health. I hope you will find this book useful as you put Ayurveda to work in your daily routine, and watch it change every aspect of your life for the better. This is Ayurveda's most fundamental purpose, and it is the deepest intent of *The Wisdom Within*.

1

MIND BODY

Are you warm and comfortable on a day when most people are wearing winter coats? Or do you begin to shiver in the slightest draft? Do you often have trouble falling asleep? Or do you drop off as soon as your head hits the pillow? Are you slow to anger and quick to forgive? Or do you often feel you've been mistreated and misunderstood? These and other questions from the program's mind body questionnaire can help you understand how the nature of the universe expresses itself in your unique mind body constitution.

Whereas conventional medicine treats each instance of a given disease in the same way, Ayurveda is based on the assumption that each patient is unique. You and I have a mind body constitution established at birth, known as our *prakruti.* According to Ayurveda—and to modern medicine— an event in the mind creates a corresponding event in the body: A fearful memory becomes adrenaline shooting into the bloodstream. Ayurveda says the interconnectedness between mind and body is accomplished at a place sandwiched between the two, where thoughts turn into matter; this place is occupied by three operating principles called *doshas.* The three doshas are Vata, Pitta, and Kapha. Although they regulate thousands of separate functions in the mind body system, they express themselves in three basic ways that shape our mind body constitution:

- Vata dosha is the principle of movement.
- Pitta dosha is the principle of metabolism.
- Kapha dosha is the principle of structure.

The doshas fundamentally influence every aspect of our lives, and understanding this influence is the basis of Ayurveda's approach to healthy living. By recognizing the importance of the doshas in your own being, you'll be able to answer that first, all-important question—"Who are you?"— in a way that reveals both your unique individuality and your oneness with all of creation.

The NATURE
of the THREE DOSHAS

What defines your essential nature? What lies at the very core of your mind body system? According to Ayurveda, you can find the answers to these questions simply by looking at your life in the everyday world.

These and other questions on the mind body questionnaire can help you understand how the nature of the universe expresses itself in your unique mind body constitution. In Ayurvedic terms, your answers on the questionnaire reveal whether your dominant dosha is Vata, Pitta, Kapha, or some combination of these three. The questionnaire also reveals any doshic imbalance that may currently be present in your system.

Vata Dosha

Vata dosha is cold and dry. It derives from the elements of space and air.

Just as the wind allows a flag to wave or a plane to fly, all motion in the body is made possible by Vata. This dosha controls the circulation of the blood, the passage of air in and out of the lungs, and even the movement of thoughts and feelings in your mind.

But, again like the wind, Vata is characterized by changeability. Of the three doshas, Vata is the most susceptible to stress of any kind, and it is the dosha that is most likely to become unbalanced.

Pitta Dosha

Pitta dosha is hot. It is primarily composed of the element of fire, which regulates the processes of metabolism, digestion, and transformation throughout the body.

Pitta regulates hunger, thirst, and body temperature. It governs all the mental processes of the mind body system, and is responsible for our ability to perceive and interpret the world accurately. The sense of sight is particularly influenced by Pitta, which is responsible for the "digestion" of visual images by the nervous system.

Simply put, Pitta is the fire that powers the body and processes everything that is taken in from the environment.

Kapha Dosha

Kapha dosha is heavy, wet, and cold. It derives from the elements of earth and water, and is responsible for the structure and lubrication of the mind body system.

Kapha sustains the strength of muscles, bones, and tendons, and balances the levels of all bodily liquids, from digestive enzymes to cerebrospinal fluid. Kapha is also responsible for the positive emotions that support us in our daily lives, such as love, compassion, and courage.

Kapha is the principle of stability. This is the dosha that "holds us together," both physically and emotionally.

Your **MIND BODY** *Type*

Vata, Pitta, and Kapha are present in every human being in different proportions. A single dosha usually predominates, but few people are purely monodoshic. Your principal dosha may be only slightly more influential than the secondary one, and sometimes, though rarely, all three doshas are present in almost equal proportion.

The universe is based on principles of change and transformation, and your doshic constitution is always in flux. Imbalances in your system almost inevitably occur, and often a particular imbalance expresses itself so strongly that the unbalanced dosha becomes, in effect, the dominant dosha in your physiology. For example, you might experience a Vata imbalance under extreme stress, although you may be a Kapha or a Pitta type under other circumstances. At that point, it becomes most important to deal with the current imbalance. For a more detailed discussion of this, refer to the section of the program on evaluating your results from the mind body questionnaire.

Mind Body Type Characteristics

VATA MIND BODY TYPES

Like air moving through space, constant motion, restless energy, and changeability are typical of the Vata nature. Balanced Vatas are happy, vibrant people who are excited by life—but that may all be different tomorrow. The only truly predictable thing about Vata types is their unpredictability.

PURE VATA

Pure Vata types usually have thin builds, though they may be of any height. Their skin tends to be dry, especially in cold weather. Joints, tendons, and veins are often visible on Vata individuals, owing to the thinness of their skin and the absence of body fat.

Emotionally, Vatas are subject to bouts of worry, and this often causes the sleep difficulties that are a common Vata characteristic. It's important, therefore, for Vatas to become aware of their needs for proper rest and nutrition. When these needs are fulfilled, the vivacious, vibrant, creative sides of the Vata nature are able to express themselves.

VATA-PITTA

Though often thin like pure Vata types, Vata-Pittas are usually more strongly built and have greater resistance to environmental influences. Their digestion gains strength from the Pitta influence, and they tend to be more stable emotionally as well.

VATA-KAPHA

A light and slender build combined with an easygoing personality is typical of this combination. Under stress, however, a Vata tendency toward anxiety can assert itself. Since both Vata and Kapha are cold doshas, this combination tends to be uncomfortable during the winter, with a vulnerability to colds and flu.

All About Vata Types

PHYSICAL

- Vatas may be either tall or short, but they usually have light, thin builds and delicate constitutions.

- Their skin is thin and dry, with veins often visible through the skin.

- In motion, they are quick and agile. Their actions are performed in short bursts of energy, and afterward they often feel exhausted.

- Because of their irregular eating habits, Vatas are often bothered by nervous stomachs and poor digestion, frequently in the form of constipation.

- Premenstrual pain is also usually related to Vata's influence.

- Vatas often complain of cold hands and feet, and they're very happy in warm climates.

EMOTIONAL / INTELLECTUAL

- Vatas are restless, creative, and enthusiastic, though there may be a lack of focus and concentration when the dosha is out of balance.

- They're quick to grasp new information, but they're likely to forget it just as easily.

- Vata types love action and excitement, but are subject to quick changes of mood and bouts of worry and anxiety.

- They spend money impulsively and their sex drives are variable.

- Vatas are usually good conversationalists, with excellent communication skills.

BALANCED VATAS

In balance, Vatas are happy, witty, alert, quick-thinking, enthusiastic, sensitive, energetic, and creative.

OUT-OF-BALANCE VATAS

Out of balance, Vatas have a tendency to be tired, sullen, forgetful, irritable, apathetic, procrastinating, anxious, and constipated.

IT IS VERY VATA TO:

- Be hungry at any time of the day or night
- Love excitement and constant change
- Go to sleep at different times every night, skip meals, and keep irregular habits in general
- Digest food well one day and poorly the next
- Display bursts of emotion that are short-lived and quickly forgotten
- Walk quickly

IN A CROWDED ELEVATOR:

If Vata types enter a crowded elevator that refuses to move, they are likely to push first one button and then another—and then suddenly decide this is neither the elevator nor the building they want to be in!

PITTA MIND BODY TYPES

Pitta is intensity. Like the element of fire from which Pitta derives, people with a predominance of this dosha draw the eyes and attention of all who come in contact with them.

PURE PITTA

Pure Pitta types are of medium build with well-proportioned features. Their hair is one of their most defining characteristics: It is often red or blond, almost always of very fine texture, and male Pittas tend toward baldness and gray hair at an early age. Their skin is often similarly fair, and it burns rather than tans in the sun. Both physically and temperamentally, Pittas are uncomfortable in hot weather.

Pittas frequently attain positions of leadership based on their public-speaking abilities and their love for challenges. Balanced Pitta types are outgoing and affectionate, but under stress they may become irritable and impatient. Anger is a characteristic emotion when Pitta is out of balance.

PITTA-VATA

Pitta-Vatas typically have strong builds, with more muscle than Vata-Pittas or pure Vatas. They are often aggressive personalities who don't hesitate to assert themselves. When out of balance, they have a tendency toward anger and insecurity.

PITTA-KAPHA

Many athletes are of this dosha combination, which combines Pitta's drive with Kapha's endurance. They usually enjoy excellent physical health. Their personalities are often dominated by Pitta's intensity, which tends to overcome the easygoing influence of the Kapha dosha.

ALL ABOUT PITTA TYPES

PHYSICAL

- Pittas are typically well-built, of medium height, and are able to maintain their weight for long periods with minimal variation.

- Pittas have excellent digestion and they often think they can eat anything and everything—but when out of balance they are vulnerable to ulcers and other gastrointestinal complaints.

- Pittas like to eat at the same times every day. If a Pitta misses a meal or is late for one, he or she is likely to become very upset.

- Because they are uncomfortable in hot weather, Pittas do not take well to prolonged exposure to the sun. They perspire heavily, and can easily become dehydrated and subject to heat fatigue.

EMOTIONAL/INTELLECTUAL

- Pittas are witty and outspoken, orderly and precise, with strong powers of concentration and sharp intellect.

- They like to persevere in a task until they feel mastery has been achieved.

- A Pitta's workplace is always clean and well-organized, but excessive Pitta can express itself in perfectionism and impatience.

- Pittas often make good teachers and excellent public speakers.

- They keep a close watch on their finances, although they may occasionally splurge on luxury items.

- Pittas have strong sex drives, and they sleep soundly, but often for only short periods of time.

BALANCED PITTAS

In balance, Pittas are confident, generous, courageous, intelligent, enterprising, warm, thoughtful, and eloquent.

OUT-OF-BALANCE PITTAS

Out of balance, Pittas have a tendency to be hostile, demanding, sarcastic, impatient, irritable, abrasive, and critical.

IT IS VERY PITTA TO:

- Feel ravenous if dinner is half an hour late
- Live by your watch and resent having your time wasted
- Wake up at night feeling hot and thirsty
- Take command of a situation or feel that you should
- Learn from experience that others find you too demanding, sarcastic, or critical at times
- Have a determined stride when you walk

IN A CROWDED ELEVATOR:

If a Pitta type enters a crowded elevator that refuses to move, he or she will probably press a button, then impatiently press the same button again several times. If the elevator doesn't start moving immediately, the distraught Pitta will decide to write a letter to the manufacturer, to the manager of the building, and perhaps even to the president of the United States!

KAPHA MIND BODY TYPES

When in balance, Kapha types have a natural strength and solidity, like mountains or redwood trees. Although Kapha is a "slow" dosha in comparison to Vata and Pitta— slow to make decisions, slow to eat, even slow to move—this is offset by Kapha's physical and intellectual power once this natural inertia is overcome.

Above all, Kaphas are strong, steady individuals. A serene, tranquil view of the world is very characteristic of Kapha types.

PURE KAPHA

Pure Kapha types are usually of solid build, with smooth skin, thick hair, and large eyes. They are often physically strong even without exercising, and they are able to endure long periods of work without feeling drained. Although they are frequently more willing to perform physical labor than Vata or Pitta types, there is also a lethargic side to the Kapha nature that can lead to complacency, overweight, and depression when the dosha is out of balance.

"Keep moving" is good advice for Kapha types. As long as they do so, Kaphas are like the tortoise who wins the race: They don't go fast, but they keep going after all the rabbits have exhausted themselves.

KAPHA-PITTA

Kapha-Pittas tend to gain weight easily and are less inclined toward activity than Pitta-Kaphas. A general roundness is characteristic of both their faces and their bodies. Although their movements are naturally rather slow, they have outstanding endurance and steady energy.

KAPHA-VATA

Kapha-Vatas are solidly built and are often athletic, but they lack the quick enthusiasm and energy that typifies pure Vata. They're often even-tempered, very relaxed individuals. Like Vata-Kaphas, they dislike cold weather and are vulnerable to respiratory infections.

ALL ABOUT KAPHA TYPES

PHYSICAL

- Kaphas are often strongly and solidly built, with thick hair and lustrous skin.

- When out of balance, Kaphas often gain weight quickly.

- Kaphas do not enjoy climates that are cool, damp, and gloomy, and they are uncomfortable when the sky is cloudy and overcast.

- They are often bothered by colds and flus during winter and early spring. But Kaphas rarely complain about the weather. In fact, they rarely complain about anything.

EMOTIONAL/INTELLECTUAL

- Although they may occasionally lose their tempers, Kaphas will put up with unpleasantness for long periods before becoming angry.

- Kaphas are neither uncomfortable with, nor particularly attached to, schedules and planned routines.

- They are mature in their approach to saving money.

- Kaphas experience deep, sound sleep and enjoy slow and easy sex drives, even dispositions, and affectionate natures. They are steady, strong, and loving people, who tend to be very tolerant and forgiving.

- Kaphas are good listeners, who prefer to speak only when they believe they have something important to say.

BALANCED KAPHAS

In balance, Kaphas are affectionate, calm, strong, hard-working, relaxed, tolerant, and graceful.

OUT-OF-BALANCE KAPHAS

Out of balance, Kaphas have a tendency to be surly, depressed, lethargic, procrastinating, sedentary, possessive, suspicious, and plodding.

IT IS VERY KAPHA TO:

- Mull things over for a long time before making a decision

- Wake up slowly, lie in bed a long time, and need coffee upon rising

- Be happy with the status quo and preserve it by conciliating others

- Respect other people's feelings (with which you feel genuine empathy)

- Seek emotional comfort from eating
- Have graceful movements, liquid eyes, and a gliding walk, even if overweight

IN A CROWDED ELEVATOR:

Although it may cause them to be late for appointments occasionally, Kaphas are blessed with an inherent ability to enjoy life, even in stressful situations. If a Kapha type enters a crowded elevator that refuses to move, he or she is likely to wait patiently for a while, then sigh and casually leave and head for a coffee shop. A delay isn't a problem—it's an opportunity to get some sweet refreshment!

THE THREE-DOSHIC TYPE

An authentic three-dosha type is quite rare. Even when Vata, Pitta, and Kapha are initially present in equal proportion, there is a tendency for one dosha to become unbalanced and dominate. Once this happens, it's quite difficult to restore the equal alignment, so the individual is in effect transformed into a two-dosha type.

Your Body's NATURAL RHYTHMS

The four seasons of the year, the lunar month, and the cyclical progression of night into day exert profound influences on the doshas, and through them on your physical and emotional condition. Learning to recognize these natural rhythms and to live in accordance with them is an important Ayurvedic principle for enjoying a balanced life.

Seasonal RHYTHMS

Ayurveda teaches that each season expresses characteristics of a specific dosha. Health concerns caused by an imbalance of Vata, Pitta, or Kapha tend to become aggravated during the season that corresponds to a particular dosha.

Vata Season

Vata season is late autumn and early winter, when the weather is cold, windy, and dry. If you are a Vata type or have a Vata imbalance, you should be particularly careful about diet and daily routine during this time of year. Chronic conditions such as arthritis tend to worsen during the Vata season.

Pitta Season

Pitta season is the hot, moist period of summer and early fall. If you are a Pitta body type or have a Pitta imbalance, you should be aware of the potential for Pitta aggravation. Tempers tend to flare and heat-related imbalances such as rashes and other skin conditions can become inflamed during the hot Pitta season.

Kapha Season

Kapha season is spring, from March to June. These months are wet and cold, and if you are a Kapha type or have a Kapha imbalance, they are a time to take special care. Colds and sinus congestion are common during the cold and rainy Kapha periods.

Daily CYCLES

Many of the body's natural fluctuations take place according to a twenty-four-hour rhythm, and you're probably already aware of these cycles. You may have noticed, for example, that despite feeling extremely tired at nine in the evening, a time when Kapha exerts its relaxing influence, you get your "second wind" around 10:00 P.M., as the stimulating presence of Pitta begins to be felt.

First Cycle of the Day

6 A.M. TO 10 A.M. — KAPHA:

Between these hours of Kapha influence, your body is likely to feel slow, heavy, and relaxed. This is a good time to exercise and get your body moving.

10 A.M. TO 2 P.M. — PITTA:

During these hours of Pitta influence, appetite and digestion are at their peak. It is the best time to have your main meal of the day.

2 P.M. TO 6 P.M. — VATA:

Mental activities and physical dexterity are most efficient in the late afternoon, a Vata-dominant time period. This is a good time for work creativity.

Second Cycle of the Day

6 P.M. TO 10 P.M. — KAPHA:

Kapha's influence tends to create a slow, relaxed mood in the evening.

10 P.M. TO 2 A.M.—PITTA:

This is the period when Pitta rejuvenates and renews the body, converting energy into warmth and rebuilding tissues as you sleep. It is the time to get rid of toxins and metabolize nutrients that have been consumed during the day, and therefore is a very important time to rest.

2 A.M. TO 6 A.M.—VATA:

During these hours of Vata's influence, the nervous system is active in the form of REM sleep, and a high level of dream activity occurs. The clearing of mental stresses and renewal of the mind occurs at this time, and it is therefore an important time to rest.

Your DAILY ROUTINE

By synchronizing your daily routine with natural ebbs and flows, and by living each moment mindfully and completely, you can bring health to your body and joy to your spirit. This schedule can serve as a guide to help you align your daily activities with nature's rhythms.

Morning

6 A.M. TO 8 A.M.
- Wake without an alarm clock
- Brush your teeth and clean your tongue if coated
- Drink a glass of warm water to encourage regular elimination
- Empty your bowels and bladder

- Massage your body, either with oil (*abhyanga*) or dry massage (*garshana*)
- Bathe
- Perform light exercise: Sun Salutation, yoga postures, breathing exercises
- Meditate
- Eat breakfast
- Take a midmorning walk

Afternoon

NOON TO 1 P.M.

- Eat lunch (the largest meal of the day)
- Sit quietly for five minutes after eating
- Walk to aid digestion (five to fifteen minutes)
- Meditate in the late afternoon

Evening

6 P.M. TO 7 P.M.

- Eat a light to moderate dinner
- Sit quietly for five minutes after eating
- Walk to aid digestion (five to fifteen minutes)

Bedtime

9:30 P.M. TO 10:30 P.M.

- Perform light activity in the evening
- Go to bed early, but at least three hours after dinner
- Do not read, eat, or watch TV in bed

2

HEALTH

When you were a child, you looked up into the night sky and found mystery and wonder. You waved to the man in the moon, you drew pictures among the stars, and if you saw a shooting star it was a chance to make a heartfelt wish. But the child's sense of the universe as a living thing doesn't last long. By the time we're nine or ten years old, most of us have learned that the moon revolves around the earth, that the earth revolves around the sun, and that the entire solar system functions in a cyclical order, like a clock. And we were also taught to think of our bodies as complex machines. When a disease or injury occurs, it can be diagnosed and treated in much the same way that mechanical failures in a car can be identified and repaired.

Ayurveda, however, has never accepted this mechanical model of the body. Instead, Ayurveda allows us to see ourselves—and the whole universe—as a subtly interconnecting network of energy and information. Ayurveda teaches that the body is in many ways like a river: flowing, always in motion, endlessly renewing itself, with each element affecting all the others and with even minute events influencing the whole.

In this view, good health is much more than the efficient functioning of the body's various parts. Health is not just the absence of disease. It is a wholeness, a supreme oneness, that erases the boundaries between our consciousness, our physical selves, and the universe around us. It combines the joy and wonder we felt as children with the knowledge we gained as we grew older, and out of this it reveals a profound truth— that just as the universe really is our extended body, our bodies also contain the universe.

THE CONSCIOUS SELF
and LOSS *of* BALANCE

If you're accustomed to thinking of your body as a living machine, you're also used to treating illness on the material level, with drugs, surgery, or perhaps radiation. But you're not just a flesh-and-blood machine that has somehow developed consciousness, nor are you a collection of chemicals that has miraculously come to life. Instead, you are a consciousness— an awareness—that has taken on the form of a physical self. With the thoughts and feelings you're having today, at this very moment, you are creating the physical body that you'll inhabit next week, next year, and even many years from now. Through the power of your perceptions, interpretations, and choices, you can strengthen health and minimize the presence of disease in your life.

Ayurveda teaches that illness originates from a loss of balance among Vata, Pitta, and Kapha, the three doshas that make up your mind body system. When this imbalance is aggravated by toxins that remain in the body as a result of improper digestion, the stage is set for the disease process to continue.

Ayurveda recognizes six specific stages of disease. The first three stages are extremely important expressions of imbalance in the mind body system, but they occur at very subtle levels. They're best understood as shifts in awareness and consciousness rather than as symptoms that can be measured with a thermometer or heard through a stethoscope. According to Ayurveda, only the three final stages of disease include the kinds of external symptoms that we usually associate with illness. As your awareness of your inner self develops, you'll be able to detect disease in its early stages and prevent a subtle imbalance from becoming a fully developed illness.

Six Stages of Disease

1. ACCUMULATION

This first stage occurs when an excessive concentration of one or more of the doshas begins to take place. This is often accompanied by a vague awareness of not feeling at your best. There may be some achiness or fatigue, but often no clearly defined symptoms are present.

2. Aggravation

The accumulated dosha begins to spread beyond its normal locations, which, in a healthy body, is the colon for Vata, the small intestine for Pitta, and the stomach for Kapha.

3. Dissemination

The unbalanced dosha disperses throughout the mind body system.

4. Localization

At this stage, the affected dosha becomes concentrated in an area of toxic accumulation, in the same way that a joint injured in childhood is susceptible to arthritis later in life. Physical sensations begin to appear, though they may be no more than a vague achiness or fatigue.

5. Manifestation

Now physical symptoms begin to appear in the specific area where the dosha has settled.

6. Disruption

Illness as it's commonly understood finally appears.

The EFFECTS of STRESS

Every thought and feeling produces a physical effect. Just by thinking about beautiful music, for example, you can relax the major muscle groups of your body and measurably slow your heartbeat. But experiencing stress instantly produces adrenaline to speed up the heart, along with many other potentially dangerous effects.

Stress lays the foundation for many physical and emotional imbalances, and it becomes especially destructive when it occurs outside your consciousness and begins to seem almost natural. So the first step in neutralizing stress lies in awareness: in recognizing the effects that daily frustrations and inconveniences are having on your mind and body.

STRESS *Test*

Here are some questions that can help you determine the level of stress in your life. If you can answer yes to most of them, you are doing a good job of dealing with the tensions of everyday living. If most of your answers are no, use the techniques that Ayurveda offers—such as yoga, meditation, massage, and exercise—to reverse the effects of stress and prevent imbalances from becoming established.

1. Did you wake up this morning feeling refreshed?
2. Did you begin the day with activities that were nurturing to your body and spirit?
3. Did you find real pleasure in your work today?
4. If you became angry, were you able to show how you really felt in a constructive way?
5. Did you spend some time outside, looking at nature with awareness and appreciation?
6. Were you able to engage in healthy activities or exercise?
7. Were you able to spend some quiet time alone?
8. If you felt tired, were you able to rest for a while?
9. Was the food you ate fresh and nutritious?

10. Were you able to eat in pleasant, unhurried surroundings?
11. Did you take your meals with company you enjoyed?
12. Did you show love today to your friends and family members?
13. Did you receive their love in return?

PURIFICATION
and REJUVENATION

When you were born, the balance point of your mind body system was precisely established—in Ayurvedic tradition, this point is called your prakruti. Over the years, deviations from this balance point occur. Stress gives rise to toxic accumulations, which in turn become the basis for disease. Ayurveda's central purpose is to eliminate these accumulations—in body, mind, and spirit—and to restore the condition of perfect balance that is your true birthright. This is what purification and rejuvenation really mean.

AMA *and* AGNI

Ayurveda refers to toxins that accumulate in the body as *ama,* a substance that is described as heavy, sticky, thick, and cold. There are many causes of ama accumulation, including unhealthy diet and a sedentary lifestyle. Even feelings of fear or hostility can eventually manifest themselves as toxic residues. A common example of ama accumulation is the white coating that's visible on your tongue in the morning, especially if you're suffering from a cold or the flu.

Agni is the mind body system's natural ama-fighter. Like the fire in a furnace that banishes cold and heats a whole house, agni is the source of power that eliminates ama from the physiology. Indeed, Ayurveda usually refers to agni through metaphors of heat, and it is sometimes called the body's digestive fire. But the Ayurvedic concept of agni carries well beyond the digestive system, and it has a profoundly spiritual component. Agni is nothing less than the transformational power of the universe. When sunlight turns a seed into a brilliant flower, when a caterpillar changes into a butterfly, when your lungs change oxygen into carbon dioxide, agni is at work.

If agni is strong and healthy within you, you're able to efficiently extract the physical, emotional, and spiritual nourishment you need from the environment, while your system naturally eliminates whatever is toxic or unnecessary. Strengthening agni and reducing ama is one of the best ways to rejuvenate body, mind, and spirit.

Purifying TECHNIQUES

Ayurveda provides a number of very practical methods for strengthening agni. You can use these techniques to stimulate metabolism and speed the elimination of toxins. Always bear in mind, however, that Ayurveda advocates balanced behavior, not extreme measures. If you experience any discomfort, feel free to discontinue or moderate the purifying techniques you've been using.

Liquid Diet

Following a liquid diet for twenty-four hours can strengthen agni and stimulate the elimination of toxins. Water, soup, juice, and blended vegetables can be taken in any quantity, while avoiding solid foods unless you begin to feel weak or uncomfortable. The frequency with which you cleanse should be determined by your dosha. Vatas can cleanse their systems with a liquid diet once each month, Pittas twice each month, and Kaphas as often as once a week.

Herbalized Hot Water

Sipping hot water flavored with cleansing herbs is a very useful ama-reducing technique. It's especially effective because it can be personalized according to your doshic needs.

If Vata or Kapha is your dominant dosha or if you currently have a Vata or Kapha imbalance, it's best to flavor your water with fresh ginger. Grate one-half teaspoon of fresh ginger and add this to a pint of very hot water. If Pitta is your dominant dosha or your imbalance, flavor a pint of hot water with one-half teaspoon of chopped licorice.

By keeping a thermos handy during the day, you can sip some of this herbalized hot water every fifteen to thirty minutes. The amount you drink is less important than the frequency, so you should have at least a few sips every hour. This may seem a bit awkward at first, but once you experience the cleansing effects of the herbalized hot water, you'll enjoy using this method.

Panchakarma

The ancient Ayurvedic procedure of *panchakarma* is also extremely effective for cleansing the entire system. Panchakarma means "five steps" in Sanskrit. It includes aroma therapy, massage, medicated enemas, herbalized steam, and the application of medicinal oils and herbal mixtures, all of which are designed to eliminate toxic accumulations from the body. And when the body is made free of toxins, the mind and the spirit are freed as well. Ideally, panchakarma is done once a year under the supervision of a qualified Ayurvedic physician.

Other Purifying Techniques

Physical and spiritual activities such as meditation, yoga, and the breathing exercise known as *pranayama* are other powerful cleansing and rejuvenating techniques. By learning to use them—and by living mindfully each day in body, in thought, and in spirit—you can banish illness and find joy in every moment of your life.

3

NUTRITION

The Ayurvedic approach to nutrition is very direct and down-to-earth. Instead of referring to calorie counts and cholesterol numbers, food is understood in terms of the tastes we actually experience when we eat. The Ayurvedic understanding of taste is very highly developed, and six distinct categories are included: sweet, sour, salty, pungent, bitter, and astringent. As you begin to broaden your choice of foods to include all of these tastes, you'll feel healthier, your enjoyment of eating will increase, and your enjoyment of living will as well.

Another important aspect of Ayurvedic nutrition is the emphasis placed on individual human differences. Good digestion, for example, depends just as much on the emotions you feel while you're eating and the awareness that you bring to the experience, as on enzymes and stomach acids.

The benefits of any food have to be considered in light of the unique needs of the person who's eating the food, as well as the attention he or she pays to the meal and pleasure he or she feels during it. By learning to listen to your body and becoming aware of its needs for both nutrition and enjoyment, you'll be able to design a diet that's exactly right for you.

A M A
and O J A S

Ama, a toxic residue left by incompletely digested substances, is created when unhealthy or unnecessary food is taken into your system. Sluggish digestion, generalized pain, poor appetite, and fatigue are some signs of its presence, and a white coating on the tongue also indicates ama. Sipping herbalized hot water throughout the day is an effective ama-reducing technique. Yoga and other forms of exercise are also beneficial, and a daily oil massage can help release accumulated toxicity through the skin.

Ojas can easily be understood as the opposite of ama. But unlike ama, ojas is not something we can touch or point to. It is an essence, something that we feel at our inner core. Ojas is produced when your entire being, including the digestive tract, is functioning well. When ojas is present, you feel physically strong and energetic, as well as emotionally confident and calm. Increasing the presence of ojas in your body creates the foundation for physical and spiritual well-being.

Ojas derives from healthy emotions as well as from good physical activities, and it is produced by experiencing each moment to the fullest. Ama, which can afflict the spirit as well as the body, is quite literally an accumulation of the past. Ojas is the present, ever vanishing yet also continuously renewing itself.

Signs and Symptoms of Ama

- Weak sense of taste
- Coating on the tongue
- Bad breath
- Poor appetite
- Indigestion
- Sour taste in the mouth
- Joint pain
- Sensation of heaviness
- Generalized aching
- Body odor
- Weakness
- Fatigue
- Lack of alertness
- Depression
- Irritability

Mental Ama

Just as ama can take the form of physical impurities, mental ama can manifest itself as negative thoughts and emotions. These too can create imbalances in mind, body, and spirit.

Causes of Mental Ama

- Negative emotions such as anger, greed, resentment, and guilt
- Psychological stresses such as financial worries, family problems, or unwholesome surroundings
- Contact with other people's negative thinking
- Exposure to violent or shocking experiences in life or in the media

Suggestions for Reducing Mental Ama

- Practice meditation.
- Spend time in nature.
- Eat light, natural, freshly prepared foods in a positive environment.
- Be pleasant, tolerant, and generous toward everyone.
- Refrain from anger and criticism.
- Act only after due reflection, not on impulse.

- Take time every day for laughter and good company.

- Wake with the sun in the morning and watch it set in the evening.

- Occasionally take a stroll in the moonlight, especially if there's a full moon.

Suggestions for Increasing Ojas

- Favor naturally warming foods such as milk, saffron, rice, and ghee (clarified butter). According to Ayurveda, such foods help to replenish ojas.

- Be patient, generous, and in every way pleasant to those around you. Find the best in people and they will find the best in you. Let others make you great, rather than trying to impress them with your greatness.

- Avoid negative emotions such as anger, worry, and regret, all of which deplete ojas. Meditation is the most effective technique for quieting the mind, reducing anxieties about the past or the future, and fostering present-moment awareness.

- Minimize the presence of drugs and stimulants in your life. Alcohol, nicotine, and caffeine are especially destructive to ojas.

- Practice moderation in all areas of your life. Rest when you're tired, eat when you're hungry, and exercise to create energy rather than exhaust it. Ayurveda also teaches that excessive sexual activity depletes ojas.

BALANCING
with the SIX TASTES

Each bite of food delivers vast amounts of information to your system. For example, the human body can perceive sweet taste in a dilution of one part to two hundred, and bitter in a dilution of one part to two million! By using taste to maintain your doshic balance, you can eat a well-balanced diet without stress and without needing a calculator to count calories or fat percentages.

Ayurveda recognizes six tastes. You're already familiar with sweet, sour, salty, and bitter, but you may need some examples of the last two—pungent and astringent. Pungent foods, such as salsa, are hot and spicy, while astringent foods, like pomegranates and beans, cause a puckering sensation in your mouth.

A well-balanced diet should include all six tastes in every meal, but since each of the tastes influences the doshas in different ways, you should adjust the proportions to your particular mind body constitution.

Sweet

The sweet taste derives from the elements of earth and water. It strengthens and adds bulk to the body, nourishes the tissues and internal organs, and brings pleasure to the experience of eating. Sweet is a predominant taste in our Western diet. When taken in excess, however, sweetness can begin to overwhelm the other tastes until it eventually comes to dominate every meal. Overweight and other health problems may result until the intake of sweet taste is reduced. Sweet foods are most beneficial for Vata and Pitta types, but should be used sparingly by Kaphas.

ELEMENTS: EARTH, WATER

EFFECT ON THE DOSHAS:

- Decreases Vata, Pitta
- Increases Kapha

BENEFITS:

- Most nutritive of all the tastes
- Builds body tissues

COMMON EXAMPLES:

- Sugar, honey, molasses, milk, butter, oils, rice, breads, pastas, sweet fruits, meats

IF TAKEN IN BALANCED AMOUNTS:

- Produces satisfaction, triggers pleasant memories of childhood, evokes feelings of love

IF TAKEN IN EXCESS:

- May promote complacency, neediness, greed, attachment

Sour

The sour taste has its foundations in the elements of earth and fire. It stimulates the appetite and the digestive processes, and facilitates elimination of wastes by the body. In small or moderate amounts, sour is beneficial to Pitta and Kapha types, but this taste is especially helpful to Vatas, whose appetites are often irregular and for whom constipation is frequently a problem.

ELEMENTS: EARTH, FIRE

EFFECT ON THE DOSHAS:

- Decreases Vata
- Increases Pitta, Kapha

BENEFITS:

- Increases appetite
- Promotes digestion
- Facilitates passing of gas
- Adds zest and flavor to other foods

COMMON EXAMPLES:

- Citrus fruits, yogurt, cheese, tomatoes, salad dressings, pickles, vinegar

IF TAKEN IN BALANCED AMOUNTS:

- Stimulates feelings of exhilaration and a desire for adventure

IF TAKEN IN EXCESS:

- May promote feelings of envy or resentment

Salty

The salty taste is based on the elements of water and fire. It cleanses the tissues, strengthens digestion, and helps relieve constipation. Salty foods are particularly useful for settling Vata imbalances, but Kaphas and Pittas can also benefit from the salty taste available in vegetables such as zucchini, cucumber, and tomatoes.

ELEMENTS: WATER, FIRE

EFFECT ON THE DOSHAS:

- Decreases Vata
- Increases Pitta, Kapha

BENEFITS:

- Mildly laxative/sedative
- Promotes digestion

COMMON EXAMPLES:

- Salt, salted meats, fish

IF TAKEN IN BALANCED AMOUNTS:

- Provides energy and strengthens courage

IF TAKEN IN EXCESS:

- May stimulate jealousy or hostility

Pungent

The pungent taste derives from the elements of fire and air. It is best taken in very small amounts by Pitta types and in moderation by Vatas, but pungent flavors such as garlic, ginger, and salsa are most beneficial for out-of-balance Kaphas. Pungent increases the appetite and benefits digestion by stimulating secretions produced by the gastrointestinal organs.

ELEMENTS: FIRE, AIR

EFFECT ON THE DOSHAS:

- Decreases Kapha
- Increases Vata, Pitta

BENEFITS:

- Stimulates digestion/secretions
- Clears congestion

COMMON EXAMPLES:

- Hot peppers, salsa, ginger, cumin, cinnamon, radishes, mustard, cloves, horseradish

IF TAKEN IN BALANCED AMOUNTS:

- Adds spice to life and creates a desire for variety

IF TAKEN IN EXCESS:

- May promote impatience, anger, sarcasm, and meanness

Bitter

The bitter taste is based on the element of air. It helps remove toxins from the body, tones and strengthens the organs, and alleviates such external problems as rashes and skin ailments. Pitta types benefit most from bitter-tasting spices such as turmeric and aloe vera, and from vegetables such as lettuce. Bitter is also helpful in treating Kapha imbalances, but it is not useful for Vata.

ELEMENTS: AIR, SPACE

EFFECT ON THE DOSHAS:

- Decreases Pitta, Kapha
- Increases Vata

BENEFITS:

- Anti-inflammatory
- Detoxifying

COMMON EXAMPLES:

- Broccoli, spinach, romaine, endive, eggplant, radishes, celery, sprouts, beets, turmeric, lemon rind, tonic water

IF TAKEN IN BALANCED AMOUNTS:

- Leads to a desire to change and grow

IF TAKEN IN EXCESS:

- May create bitterness and frustration

Astringent

The astringent taste derives from the elements of air and earth. All three doshas can benefit from astringent in very small amounts, but it is more useful for Kapha and Pitta than for Vata. It has a generally drying and constricting effect on bodily functions, and it reduces secretions produced by the gastrointestinal organs. Beans, lentils, apples, and pears are astringent-tasting foods, and most medicines are also astringent.

ELEMENTS: AIR, EARTH

EFFECT ON THE DOSHAS:

- Decreases Pitta, Kapha
- Increases Vata

BENEFITS:

- Drying effect can benefit Kapha
- Reduces bloating and biliousness

COMMON EXAMPLES:

- Beans, lentils, tea, apples, pears, broccoli, pomegranates, persimmons, cabbage, cauliflower, dark leafy greens

IF TAKEN IN BALANCED AMOUNTS:

- Fosters introspection, wit, humor

IF TAKEN IN EXCESS:

- Aggravates feelings of insecurity and cynicism

CHOOSING
the right DIET

Ayurveda recommends following a diet that is specifically tailored to balance your doshic makeup—but this doesn't mean you should approach eating in a restricted or worry-filled state of mind. Enjoyment of food is the single most important Ayurvedic principle of diet, and the pleasure of any meal is as important as its nutritional content. No matter what mind body type you are, virtually nothing needs to be strictly eliminated. Instead, certain foods should be favored and others should be reduced.

Vata-Balancing Diet

Vata is the air dosha, and Vata types tend to be flighty in their habits. When out of balance they often eat quickly, irregularly, or not at all. The Vata-balancing diet emphasizes foods that are substantial and nutritious rather than just "fast" or "convenient." By following this diet, Vatas can regain their enjoyment of eating as well as their doshic balance.

RECOMMENDATIONS

- Favor foods that are warm, heavy, oily, and thoroughly cooked. Minimize foods that are cold, dry, light, and raw.

- Favor foods that are sweet, sour, and salty. Minimize foods that are spicy, bitter, and astringent.

- Eat larger quantities, but not more than you can digest easily.

- Dairy: All dairy products pacify Vata.

- Sweeteners: All sweeteners are acceptable.

- Oils: All oils pacify Vata; sesame oil is especially recommended.

- Grains: Rice and wheat are very good. Reduce barley, corn, millet, buckwheat, rye, and oats.

- Fruits: Favor sweet, sour, or heavy fruits, such as oranges, bananas, grapes, and dried fruits.

- Vegetables: Beets, cucumbers, carrots, asparagus, and sweet potatoes are good. They should be cooked rather than eaten raw.

- Spices: Cardamom, cumin, ginger, cinnamon, salt, cloves, mustard seed, and small quantities of black pepper are all acceptable.

- Nuts and seeds: All nuts are acceptable in small amounts; almonds are best.

- Beans: Reduce all beans, except tofu and split mung-bean soup.

- Meat and fish (for nonvegetarians): Chicken, turkey, and seafood are acceptable, but beef should be minimized.

Although oily, heavier, sweeter, and richer foods are usually recommended to pacify Vata, excessive weight gain may make lighter foods with Vata-pacifying qualities more desirable.

RECOMMENDATIONS

- Heavier, sweeter, and richer foods are usually recommended for pacifying Vata, but certain lighter foods can also benefit Vata imbalances. As always, try to eat only when your hunger is strong, and be sure your meals are well-prepared, flavorful, and served in a quiet, pleasant environment.

VATA-LIGHT FOODS

- Grains: Rice, wheat, and oats are excellent, but they should be prepared with reduced amounts of oil or sweeteners.
- Sweeteners: All sweeteners may be used, but in reduced amounts. Cooking with honey is not recommended.
- Dairy: Favor low-fat milk and low-fat yogurt, while reducing quantities of cheese and cream.
- Oils: Small quantities of oil can be used, with the exception of coconut oil. Small amounts of clarified butter (ghee) are also acceptable.
- Legumes: Green or yellow mung beans and red lentils are best. To prepare them, mix one part dried beans with two parts water and boil to the consistency of soup.
- Vegetables: These should be well-cooked, and are best

eaten in soups, casseroles, and stews. Carrots, zucchini, asparagus, spinach, tomato, and artichokes are best.

- Fruits: Favor sweet, ripe fruits in season. Figs, pineapples, grapes, apricots, sweet oranges, papayas, and small amounts of raisins are acceptable.

- Spices: Warmer and sweeter spices are best, including ginger, cumin, cinnamon, and cardamom. Salt, lemon juice, and tamarind are also acceptable in small amounts.

Pitta-Balancing Diet

Pitta is associated with heat, and Pitta people often believe that their digestive fires can consume virtually anything. This tendency of Pittas to overestimate what their systems can handle leads to ulcers and other gastrointestinal problems. The Pitta-balancing diet cools the system, while avoiding foods that are excessively hot or spicy.

RECOMMENDATIONS

- Favor foods that are cool or warm. Minimize foods that are steaming hot.

- Favor tastes that are sweet, bitter, or astringent.

- Minimize spicy, salty, or sour tastes.

PITTA FOODS

- Dairy: Milk, butter, and ghee are good for pacifying Pitta. Reduce yogurt, cheese, and sour cream.

- Sweeteners: All sweeteners are good except honey and molasses.

- Oils: Olive, sunflower, and coconut oils are best. Reduce sesame, almond, and corn oil.

- Grains: Wheat, white rice, barley, and oats are good. Reduce corn, rye, millet, and brown rice.

- Fruits: Favor sweet fruits, such as grapes, cherries, melons, berries, and avocados. Reduce sour fruits, such as grapefruits, olives, and pineapples.

- Vegetables: Favor asparagus, cucumbers, potatoes, sweet potatoes, broccoli, and cauliflower. Reduce hot peppers, tomatoes, carrots, beets, onions, garlic, radishes, spinach, and mustard greens.

- Beans: Reduce all beans, except tofu and split mung dahl.

- Nuts and seeds: Favor coconut; reduce all other nuts and seeds, except pumpkin and sunflower seeds.

- Spices: Cinnamon, coriander, cardamom, and fennel are acceptable. Reduce ginger, cumin, black pepper, fenugreek, salt, and mustard. Chili peppers and cayenne should also be avoided.

- Meat and fish (for nonvegetarians): Chicken, pheasant, and turkey are preferable. Beef, seafood, and eggs should be minimized.

Kapha-Balancing Diet

Kapha is a cold, moist dosha, related to the elements of earth and water. Kapha-balancing foods are light and warm to counter Kapha's tendency toward heaviness and inertia. Spicy foods are also beneficial, since they tend to speed up the often-sluggish Kapha digestion.

RECOMMENDATIONS

- Favor foods that are light, dry, and warm. Minimize foods that are heavy, oily, and cold.

- Favor small, light meals at breakfast and dinner, which can include lightly cooked vegetables and fruits.

- Favor foods that are pungent, bitter, and astringent. Spicy foods promote better digestion.

- Minimize foods that are sweet, salty, and sour.

KAPHA FOODS

- In general, avoid dairy products, except low-fat milk.

- Fruit: Lighter fruits, such as apples and pears, are best. Reduce heavy or sour fruits, such as oranges, bananas, and pineapples.

- Sweeteners: Honey is excellent for reducing Kapha, but sugar products should be minimized.

- Beans: All beans are acceptable except soybeans and tofu.

- Nuts and seeds: Reduce all nuts. Favor sunflower and pumpkin seeds.

- Grains: Most grains are acceptable, especially barley and millet. Reduce wheat and rice.

- Vegetables: All are acceptable, except tomatoes, cucumbers, sweet potatoes, and zucchini.

- Spices: All are acceptable except salt.

- Meat and fish (for nonvegetarians): White meat of chicken or turkey is acceptable, as is seafood. Minimize red meat.

The Detox Diet

When digestion of food is weak and incomplete, an accumulation of ama can occur. Ama blocks the flow of energy throughout the body, and is the basis of all disease. Eliminating ama, therefore, is a major goal of Ayurvedic medicine, because toxic accumulations must be identified and cleansed from the system before steps to balance the doshas can be effective.

RECOMMENDATIONS

The quality and type of food you eat, the environment in which it's prepared, and the setting in which it's eaten can all influence the process of digestion.

Guidelines for the detox diet help promote strong digestion and prevent the accumulation of toxins. This diet is especially recommended at the turn of fall, winter, and spring.

Vata types should follow the diet for one to two weeks, while Pittas may use it for up to a month. Kaphas can benefit from the diet for even longer periods, as it most closely resembles a Kapha-pacifying program.

Remember that your approach to this way of life should

be effortless and compassionate, without a sense of strain or rigidity. If this is the case, you'll soon begin to experience tranquillity of mind and lightness of heart, together with more energy and natural enthusiasm for life.

Detox Foods

- All foods should be freshly prepared, nutritious, and appetizing.
- Favor freshly steamed or very lightly sautéed vegetables.
- Fresh fruits are acceptable.
- Dairy is not recommended on the detox diet.
- Favor lighter grains such as barley or basmati rice.
- Oils should be kept to a minimum.
- Avoid canned foods and leftovers.
- Avoid fried foods, cold foods and drinks, and fermented foods and drinks such as vinegar, cheeses, and alcohol.
- Beans: Favor mung dahl, which is easiest to digest.
- Avoid most nuts, but small amounts of sunflower, pumpkin, or sesame seeds can be taken.
- Avoid refined sugar. Small amounts of honey may be taken, but honey should not be heated or used in cooking.
- For the period of the detox program try to avoid animal products, including fish, fowl, and beef.

The Sattvic Diet

The Sanskrit word *sattva* is often translated as "purity," and a diet consisting of foods that purify your system with a minimum effort on your body's part may be called truly sattvic. Choosing to follow a sattvic diet may require you to make some adjustments in your eating habits, but the benefits to your physical, emotional, and spiritual health can make it well worthwhile.

RECOMMENDATIONS

- Eat fresh food appropriate to the season and to your geographical area. If possible, seek out fruits, vegetables, and dairy products that have been grown in the same air that you breathe and have been nourished by the same water that you drink.

- Have your largest meal at lunch, when your digestion is strongest. Breakfast is optional, and should be your smallest meal. Dinner should be of moderate size, so that it can be digested before you sleep.

- Don't snack, and eat your meals at the same time every day. This will help your body create a strong digestive rhythm.

- Eat alone or with friends or family. Negative emotions on the part of anyone involved with your meal can harm digestion and create ama.

- Be grateful for the food you eat. Enjoy it in an atmosphere of respect and love.

Sattvic Foods

A sattvic diet should include:

- Light, easily digested food
- Fresh vegetables
- Spring water
- Milk
- Ghee (clarified butter)
- Fruits and fruit juices
- Rice
- Sesame and almonds
- Sweet taste in general
- All six tastes
- Moderate portions of food

A sattvic diet should not include:

- Meat, poultry, and fish
- Oily or heavy foods
- Eggs and cheese
- Leftovers and processed foods
- Excess of sour and salty tastes
- Large portions of food

Recommended Tastes

- Bitter taste reduces ama and pungent taste destroys it.
- Astringent taste is generally neutral in its effect on ama.

- Sweet, salty, and sour tastes may increase ama accumulation.

- Bitter spices such as turmeric, coriander, and dill are useful ama reducers.

- Hot spices such as cayenne, black pepper, dry ginger, and mustard are very useful in burning up ama, but should be used cautiously by Pitta types.

- Fresh ginger is not as heating as the dry form, and should be used in greater quantities.

Weight Control

As in so many areas of Ayurveda, the process of arriving at a healthy weight begins by learning to listen to your own inner wisdom. As a first step to attaining the weight that's best for you, ask yourself these questions:

- When do you really feel your best?
- When do you feel most energetic?
- When do you look at yourself and like what you see?

Honest and heartfelt answers to these questions depend on your ability to distance yourself from the guilts, worries, and criticisms that are constantly associated with the issue of weight in our society. Once you begin to understand your body's true needs, you'll be able to fulfill them without stress or a painful sense of self-deprivation. You'll even enjoy an occasional chocolate sundae!

4

EXERCISE

The human body is meant to be used. Everyone can benefit from appropriate physical activity, but to be effective in Ayurvedic terms an exercise program should begin with an understanding of your mind body type. Taking your mind body type into consideration, you can design a program of activity to maintain the unique proportion of Vata, Pitta, and Kapha in your system.

As it does with all activities, Ayurveda emphasizes the need for exercise to be enjoyable. Physical activity should produce energy and alertness, not exhaustion. Once this is understood, you can approach exercise with the same effortless joy that is so apparent in children, who love play for its own sake, but who also have the good sense to stop playing when they feel tired. You can rediscover this playful spirit at any age, and you can retain it throughout your life.

EXERCISE
for the DOSHAS

To gain maximum benefit from exercise, you should choose activities that balance your particular physiology. If you haven't been exercising regularly, however, it's a good idea to start with a light level of activity regardless of your mind-body type. Consult your health-care provider before beginning any exercise program.

Vata

Because Vata dosha can easily be thrown out of balance by overexertion, Vata types should favor light exercises that emphasize balance and stretching. If Vata is your predominant dosha, easy walking, bicycling, yoga, and dance are best suited for you.

Pitta

Pitta types enjoy challenges, but they also tend to push themselves too hard. Brisk walking, jogging, skiing, bicycling, and swimming are good Pitta activities, but remember to approach them as playful enjoyments rather than intense competitions.

Kapha

Kapha types require vigorous exercise and activities that emphasize endurance. Running, bicycling, swimming, weight training, and aerobics are appropriate for Kaphas. Although they're sometimes slow getting started, Kaphas have excellent stamina and can benefit from the experience of friendly athletic competition.

YOGA

In Sanskrit, yoga means "union," and its true purpose is to create oneness among body, mind, and spirit. This ancient system is easily adapted to a modern lifestyle, and it offers many practical techniques for enjoying lifelong health.

Although many people in the West still associate yoga with difficult postures and trancelike states of mind, that is a misconception. In practicing the postures of yoga, you should be building an attitude of kindness and respect for your body. Force or strain is contrary to the essence of yoga, which above all else seeks to foster balance, awareness of the body, and an overall sense of well-being.

Yoga postures change the chemistry of muscle tissue by expanding and contracting the muscles themselves. The postures massage, stretch, and tone the body's muscles and internal organs. With the stretching of your muscles, the motion of your breath, and the movement of your spine, you can build strength, stamina, flexibility, and heightened awareness.

The
SUN SALUTATION

The Sun Salutation, a series of twelve yoga postures performed in a fluid sequence, is a complete Ayurvedic exercise that simultaneously integrates all the elements of the physiology—mind, body, and breath. It is one of Ayurveda's most powerful and effective exercises, and it has been called the essence, or "nectar," of yoga postures. Although there are thousands of poses in the yogic tradition, this simple progression is the one exercise routine everyone should learn. Ayurvedic tradition teaches that anyone who performs the Sun Salutation every day is sure to live a long and healthy life.

As you perform the Sun Salutation's twelve postures, try to synchronize each motion with your breath. Move smoothly into each pose, breathing fully and easily so that one complete cycle takes about a minute. Start slowly, and listen to your body as you gradually increase the number of Sun Salutation cycles. Stop if you notice that you are breathing and perspiring heavily or feeling too tired. If this occurs, lie down and rest for a minute or two. With regular performance, your capacity will naturally increase.

Although this exercise is highly beneficial regardless of your body type, variations do apply to each dosha. Vata types should perform the Sun Salutation slowly and steadily, Pitta types at a moderate pace, and Kaphas should try to move more quickly. Depending upon your body type and how you are feeling on a particular day, you may perform two to twelve complete cycles of the Sun Salutation.

SUN SALUTATION
Postures

SALUTATION POSE

Begin by standing tall with the feet together in a parallel position, hip distance apart. Stand evenly on both feet and lengthen your spine. Place the palms of your hands together in front of your chest. Lift the chest slightly and expand your ribs as you look straight ahead, eyes soft. Take a deep breath in and then exhale slowly.

SKY-REACHING POSE

Now inhale and slowly extend your arms over your head. Lift and expand the chest as you continue lengthening the spine, while allowing your head and eyes to look upward. Breathe evenly and calmly.

HAND TO FOOT POSE

As you exhale, bend at the hips and move your body forward and down, bringing your hands toward your feet. Try not to lock your legs; instead, allow your knees to soften or bend freely. Lengthen your spine and avoid collapsing the chest or overrounding the upper back. Keep your shoulders soft and relaxed, and remember, increased flexibility and suppleness come with regular practice.

EQUESTRIAN POSE

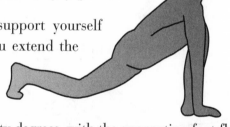

Now inhale and support yourself with both hands as you extend the left leg back and drop the knee to the ground. The right knee should bend no more than ninety degrees, with the supporting foot flat on the floor. Extend or lift the spine and open your chest as you look upward.

MOUNTAIN POSE

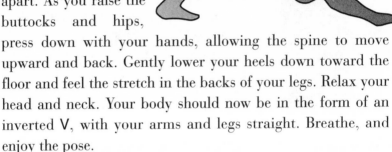

As you exhale, lift the left knee off the ground and bring your right leg backward until it's even with the left. Legs should be hip width apart. As you raise the buttocks and hips, press down with your hands, allowing the spine to move upward and back. Gently lower your heels down toward the floor and feel the stretch in the backs of your legs. Relax your head and neck. Your body should now be in the form of an inverted V, with your arms and legs straight. Breathe, and enjoy the pose.

EIGHT LIMBS POSE

Gently lower both knees to the ground and slowly slide the body down at an angle as you bring the chest and chin to the ground. All eight limbs— feet, knees, chest, hands, and chin—touch the floor. The buttocks remain slightly raised. Hold this very briefly and then continue to move into the next pose.

COBRA POSE

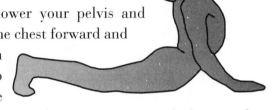

As you inhale, lower your pelvis and then lift and expand the chest forward and up as you press down with your hands. Keep the elbows close to the body and continue to extend your spine upward. Open and widen the chest and move the shoulders down and away from the ears. Let the upper back widen and lengthen as well. Be careful not to initiate this pose with the head or attempt to lift the body with your neck. Nor should you push off with your arms, because this can cause strain in your lower back. The lift should be primarily from your back and chest.

MOUNTAIN POSE

Now you'll begin reversing the order of the poses, rising once again into the mountain pose. Begin by exhaling. Raise the buttocks and hips, press down with your hands, and allow the spine to move upward and back. Stretch the heels down toward the ground and lengthen through the backs of your legs. Let your head and neck be relaxed and free. Your body should once again be in the form of an inverted V, with your arms and legs straight.

EQUESTRIAN POSE

Inhale and swing the right leg forward between your hands, bending
the knee at a ninety-
degree angle—foot flat
on the floor. The left
leg stays extended back, knee to the ground. Extend or lift the
spine and open your chest as you look upward.

HAND TO FOOT POSE

As you exhale, step forward with the
left leg and continue to bend the body forward and down. Lengthen the entire spine,
and avoid collapsing your chest or overrounding the upper back. If possible, both
hands remain on the ground. Let your knees
bend freely, and keep your elbows and
shoulders relaxed.

SKY-REACHING POSE

Inhaling, lift your arms upward using the muscles of your upper back, as you lift the chest forward and up. Continue to open and expand the chest as you extend your arms over your head. Lengthen your spine and allow your head and eyes to look upward. Keep your breathing smooth, deep, and continuous.

SALUTATION POSE

Exhale as you lower the arms and bring the palms of your hands together in front of your chest. Stand tall with the feet together in a parallel position, hip distance apart. Lift your chest and expand your ribs as you look straight ahead, eyes soft. Take a deep breath in and then exhale slowly.

This completes one cycle of the Sun Salutation. On subsequent cycles, alternate which foot extends back and which swings forward in the Equestrian pose. For example, in your second cycle, your right leg would extend backward as your left leg comes into a ninety-degree angle.

After you have completed the desired number of Sun Salutations, lie flat on your back with your spine resting evenly on the ground. Straighten your legs, lengthening them away from your pelvis; then relax, and let them fall open to the sides. Let your arms rest loosely beside your body, palms up. Close your eyes and allow your body to relax completely for at least a minute or two. This pose, known as the Awareness pose, invigorates and refreshes both the body and the mind, relieves fatigue, and soothes the entire system.

BREATHING

From the first breath you draw as a newborn baby through the last breath you exhale at the end of your life, breathing is the defining activity of your very being. In Ayurveda, the Sanskrit word *prana* refers to the vital life force, the primary energy of the universe that animates all living things. As you breathe, you bring this life force into your body.

Pranayama is the Ayurvedic science of breath. By practicing the pranayama breathing exercises described below, you can learn to consciously activate and direct the life force as it enters and becomes part of you.

Vata-Calming Exercises

NADI SHODHANA

Nadi Shodhana, which means "channel purification" in Sanskrit, is alternate-nostril breathing. By balancing your breath and by focusing your attention on your breathing, this technique can help soothe Vata's effects on both mind and body.

To begin, sit in a comfortable chair with your back straight and your feet flat on the floor. Gently draw your attention to your breath.

Place the thumb of your right hand beside your right nostril . . . and your two middle fingers beside your left nostril. Gently close the right nostril with your thumb as you slowly exhale through the left nostril.

Now inhale easily through the left nostril. Close the left nostril with the two middle fingers and exhale out the right nostril. Then inhale easily through the right nostril. . . .

Once again, gently close the right nostril with your thumb, as you slowly exhale through the left nostril. Now inhale easily through the left nostril. Close the left nostril with the two middle fingers and exhale out the right nostril. Then inhale easily through the right nostril.

This concludes two cycles of Nadi Shodhana. Notice the pause between each breath and be sure to keep your breathing long, slow, and refined. In general, perform three complete cycles of Nadi Shodhana with each nostril over a period of four to five minutes.

After completing any breathing exercise, take a few moments to rest with your eyes closed, breathing slowly and evenly, drawing your attention inward. Let your awareness be on your body and on any sensations that you're experiencing. This rest period is an important part of all pranayama techniques.

BHRIMARI

Bhrimari, which means "bumblebee" in Sanskrit, can help quiet your mind when you're anxious or upset. Like Nadi Shodhana, this technique can be used to overcome insomnia and promote restful sleep.

Sit in a comfortable chair with your back straight and your feet flat on the floor. Take a deep breath, and then make a low humming deep in your throat as you slowly exhale through your nose. Now inhale again through your nose, and repeat the humming sound as you exhale. In general, perform five cycles of Bhrimari over a period of two to three minutes.

Pitta-Cooling Exercises

UJJAYI

Ujjayi, which means "control through expansion" in Sanskrit, is a breathing exercise for cooling the back of your throat. It is also an efficient way of bringing oxygen into your lungs.

Begin by whispering the word *ha*. Focus your attention on the point where this breath originates in your throat. Now close your mouth, breathe through your nose, and without vocalizing, create this same soft whispering sound that comes when you breathe from the back of your throat.

As you continue to breathe you'll be able to feel air striking the roof of your mouth. Keep the sound smooth and light. Close your eyes and continue to breathe easily for a few breaths. There is no need to force your breath in or out.

The practice of Ujjayi helps to expand, lengthen, and deepen your breath. It oxygenates the blood and it is both calming and invigorating. You can use this whispering breath as you move through any of your yoga postures. In general, perform Ujjayi for five cycles over a period of two to three minutes.

SITALI

Sitali, which means "cooling" in Sanskrit, is useful for restoring balance whenever you're feeling angry or physically overheated.

Begin by curling your tongue into a tunnel shape, or if you cannot do this easily, use a sipping sound as you inhale through your mouth—like sipping through a straw. Exhale through your nose or from the back of your throat as in the Ujjayi breathing exercise.

Now, create the sipping sound on inhale. Feel the cooling sensation of your breath—and then exhale through your nose. Continue to repeat this breathing cycle, easily and smoothly. In general, perform Sitali for five cycles over a period of two to three minutes.

Kapha-Energizing Exercises

KAPALABHATI

Kapalabhati, which means "lustrous head" in Sanskrit, stimulates Kapha and draws energy into the mind body system. To perform Kapalabhati, sit comfortably on the ground or in a chair with your back straight and your feet flat on the floor.

Begin by exhaling forcefully through your nose, vigorously contracting your diaphragm or belly. Emphasize the exhale while just allowing the inhale to passively come in. Continue to emphasize your exhale as you breathe evenly.

In general, perform three cycles of ten breaths each, with a minute of slow, deep breathing between each cycle. You may also just take a few breaths and then rest between each cycle. Be sure to stop the exercise or reduce the number of repetitions if you feel light-headed or uncomfortable.

B HASTRIKA

Bhastrika, which means "bellows breath" in Sanskrit, is a vigorous exercise for stimulating the sluggishness of Kapha.

Begin by sitting comfortably on the floor or in a chair with both feet flat on the floor. Now inhale and exhale quickly and forcefully through your nose. In this exercise you are emphasizing the forcefulness of both the inhale and the exhale. As you breathe, try to keep your body relaxed except for the vigorous movement of your diaphragm and belly.

In general, you should inhale and exhale vigorously for one full minute. But be sure to stop the exercise or reduce the number of repetitions if you experience any discomfort or dizziness.

Prana-Enhancing Exercises

The concept that Ayurveda calls prana is found in many philosophical systems. In traditional Chinese medicine, for example, it is known as chi. Ayurveda teaches that prana is the life force, the energizing principle derived from the five elements that are the basic components of the universe—earth, water, fire, air, and space. There are a number of highly beneficial activities you can do every day to draw energy into your life from these five elements.

EARTH

Let your bare feet touch the earth at least once a day, even if it's only for a few minutes.

WATER

View the ocean, or another natural body of water. If you can, let the water come in contact with your body, or at least with your hands or feet.

FIRE

Feel the warmth of the sun on your bare skin every day.

AIR

Inhale the breath of plants. If possible, walk among plants and flowers at sunset, when the air is suffused with their scents.

SPACE

Gaze at the stars and the moon.

5

MEDITATION

If you can bring only one Ayurvedic technique into your life, meditation should unquestionably be your choice. Through the practice of meditation—whether it's mindfulness meditation or primordial sound meditation using a mantra or a guided meditation—you can create an internal reference point of spirit rather than ego. You can enter the silent spaces between your thoughts, the gap in which ego-based concerns disappear and the thinker, the process of thinking, and the object of thought are revealed to be one.

A state of "restful alertness" may be the best way to describe meditative experience. As meditation becomes a part of your daily routine, this state will naturally become a kind of internal compass, to help clarify and deepen every aspect of your life. By centering yourself at this internal reference point on a regular basis, you can dramatically strengthen the influence of spirit in your life.

MINDFULNESS
Meditation

Mindfulness meditation is a very powerful technique for entering a state of restful alertness, and it's also one of the easiest and most accessible forms of meditation. Simply by focusing your awareness on your breathing, mindfulness meditation quiets the everyday static of your thoughts.

It's best to practice this technique twice each day, in the morning and in the early evening. Create a peaceful, pleasant space for yourself where you won't be disturbed, and set aside 20–30 minutes for your meditation.

Practicing Mindfulness Meditation

1. Close your eyes. (10 seconds)
2. Gently focus awareness on your breathing. As you inhale and exhale, simply observe your breath. (30 seconds)
3. Just remain aware of your breathing, without trying to alter it in any way. (15 seconds)
4. As you observe your breath, it may vary in speed, rhythm, or depth. It may even seem to stop for a time. Without resisting, calmly observe these changes. (1 minute)

5. At times your attention may drift to a thought passing through your mind, to a physical sensation in your body, or to some distraction in the environment. Whenever you notice that you are not observing your breath, gently refocus your attention. (1 minute)

6. Relinquish any expectations you may have during the practice of this technique. If you find yourself being drawn to a particular feeling, mood, or expectation, treat this as you would any other thought. Gently return your awareness to your breath. (20–30 minutes)

7. Open your eyes slowly, returning attention to the sights and sounds around you.

PRIMORDIAL SOUND
Meditation

Primordial sounds are the natural vibrations that structure the universe. They are the seed sounds of every language. We can hear them in the songs of birds, the rushing of streams, the crashing of waves, and in the whispering breezes in the leaves of a tree. According to Ayurveda, listening to primordial sounds restores our sense of connection to the whole and enlivens our inner healing energy.

Primordial sound meditation makes use of the root sounds of the Sanskrit alphabet to create mantras. These are syllables that don't carry meaning in the sense of everyday speech. Because they are free of the associations that accompany the words we normally use, primordial sounds temporarily interrupt our otherwise continuous internal dialogue.

Primordial sound meditation is taught by a trained

instructor. The mantra is then used as a subtle vibration to create a quieting resonance in the mind. With practice, a genuine experience of inner silence can be achieved.

GUIDED
Meditation

Once you've learned to enter the state of restful alertness, you can use mental imagery to activate attention and intention at subtle levels, and to energize the deepest healing processes of your body.

Here are three guided meditations that appear in the program. Before making use of them or of any guided meditation, it's best to spend 10 minutes in mindfulness or primordial sound meditation. And when the imaging experience has been completed, remain in a relaxed state for 5 minutes before opening your eyes.

Closing the Gap

Imagine two candles standing about three feet apart on a table in front of you. They appear to be separate and independent, yet the light they cast fills the room with photons. The entire space between them is bridged by light, and therefore, at the quantum level, there is no real separation.

Now imagine that you've carried one of the candles outside into the night. Imagine that you're holding it up against a background of stars.

The pinpoints of light in the sky may be billions of light-years away, yet at the quantum level each star is connected to your candle as the second candle in the room was. The stars and your candle are bound together by waves of energy that cross the space between them.

As you look at the candle and the distant stars, photons of light from each are landing on the retinas of your eyes. The photons trigger flashes of electrochemical discharge that belong to a different vibratory frequency from visible light, but they are part of the same electromagnetic field. You, therefore, are another candle—or even a star—whose local concentration of matter and energy is one outcropping in the infinite field that surrounds and supports you.

Piercing the Mask of Matter

Look down at your hand and examine it closely. Trace its familiar lines and furrows, feel the supple flesh and the hardness of bone underneath.

This is the hand your senses report to you—it's a material object. But you're about to experience your hand from a perspective that's quite beyond the reach of your senses.

Now close your eyes and hold the image of your hand in your mind's eye. Imagine that you are examining it through a supremely powerful microscope whose lens can penetrate to the most basic levels of matter and energy. Even at the lowest power, you no longer see your hand as a surface of smooth flesh. Instead, it appears as a vast collection of individual cells loosely bound by connective tissue.

When you adjust the microscope to a higher power, you see individual atoms of hydrogen, carbon, oxygen, and other elements. But these atoms have no solidity whatsoever. The microscope reveals them to be nothing more than ghostly, vibrating shadows.

As you arrive at the boundary between matter and energy, you see that the subatomic particles that make up each atom are not really particles at all. They are just energy trails, like the traces of light left by a Fourth of July sparkler when you wave it in the dark. Each of these energy trails is a fleeting quantum event, dying out as soon as it's noticed.

Now you're sinking even deeper into quantum space. All light disappears, replaced by yawning chasms of black emptiness. But then, far away on the horizon of your vision, you see a last flash—like the farthest, faintest star visible in the night sky. Hold that flash in your mind, for it is the last remnant of matter or energy detectable by any scientific instrument. As the blackness closes in, you are in a place where not just matter and energy have vanished, but space and time as well.

You have left behind the concept of your hand as a space-time event, and you have discovered that, like all space-time events, your hand has an origin in a deeper dimension. Here there's no such thing as "before" or "after," no concept of "big" or "small." Here your hand exists both before the big bang of creation and after the universe comes to an end. You have arrived at the prequantum region that has no dimensions and all dimensions. You are everywhere—and you are nowhere.

Has your hand ceased to exist? No, because you haven't really gone anywhere. It's just that the whole notion of space and time no longer applies. Your hand still exists at all the levels you have traversed—cellular, molecular, atomic, sub-atomic, quantum—and it is connected by invisible intelligence to the place where you now find yourself. Each level you've passed through is a layer of transformation, completely different from the one above or below it, but it is only here at the quantum level that all matter is reduced to its common origin. Here there is nothing but pure energy, information, and creative potential.

Now you can examine your hand with a new understanding. It is the stepping-off point for a dizzying descent into the dance of life—where the dancers disappear if you approach too near and the music fades away into the silence of eternity. The dance is forever, and the dance is you.

Breathing the Field

Sit comfortably in a chair with your eyes closed. Gently and slowly inhale through your nostrils, imagining as you do so that you are drawing the air from a distant star, a point infinitely far away. See the air gently coming to you from the edge of the universe. Feel it coolly suffusing your body.

Now slowly and easily exhale, sending every atom of air back to its source: the star infinitely far away. If you aren't a good visualizer, don't worry; just hold the word *infinite* in your mind as you breathe. The purpose is to feel each breath coming to you from the quantum field, and at a subtle level, this is exactly what's happening.

6

AROMA THERAPY

Of all the senses, smell has the greatest ability to reach the sources of our memories and our unconscious responses. This is because receptors in the nose are direct extensions of the hypothalamus area of the brain, which controls many vital life functions as well as emotional states such as happiness, fear, and sexual arousal.

Because the sense of smell provides direct contact with the hypothalamus, aroma therapy has important uses in medicine. Aromas can be used to trigger a process whereby the brain generates healing impulses that have been linked to certain smells. This process also has an important role in Ayurvedic health care. Using aromas that are specifically matched to Vata, Pitta, or Kapha, we can restore balance to the doshas and maintain health throughout the mind body system.

AROMA THERAPY
for the DOSHAS

Vata

Vata is based on the element of air, and like the wind, it is subject to quick changes of intensity and direction. To pacify Vata, select aromas that create an atmosphere of relaxation and tranquillity.

PACIFYING AROMAS:

Floral, fruity, warm, sweet, sour

FOUND IN:

Basil, orange, geranium, clove, rose

BENEFITS:

Calms Vata restlessness and anxiety, promotes sleep, and stabilizes digestion

Pitta

Pitta derives from the element of fire. When out of balance, it can foster heated emotions such as anger and impatience. Cooling aromas can reduce emotional intensity and prevent the onset of digestive problems that often accompany a Pitta imbalance.

Cooling and sweet

Sandalwood, mint, rose, and jasmine

Soothes anger, impatience, or jealousy typical of unbalanced Pitta, and relieves emotionally based digestive problems

Kapha

Kapha derives from the elements of earth and water. It is a heavy, cold dosha, and it's responsible for creating structure in the body. Kapha responds best to warm, stimulating, energizing aromas, which help balance a tendency toward inertia and sluggishness.

PACIFYING AROMAS:

Stimulating, spicy, aromatic

FOUND IN:

Juniper, eucalyptus, camphor, clove, marjoram

BENEFITS:

Reduces retention of fats and fluids, and stimulates the often sluggish Kapha metabolism

7

SIGHT

As much as eighty-five percent of our total sensory input reaches the brain through the eyes, and for most people the sense of sight is their primary source of information about the world. This can be both a help and a hindrance in maintaining balance among the doshas. The visual static that's always present in our lives can be stressful, so it's important to counteract this with sights that relax and strengthen your mind body system. Discovering these positive visual experiences can utterly transform your feelings for the world around you, as if you've at last turned on a light after many hours in a dark room. It's all just a matter of learning to see with intention and awareness.

If you're ill, seeing beautiful things can speed the healing process. Hospital patients whose rooms overlook a pond or a group of trees seem to get well faster than those who can see only a parking lot, and there is evidence that sight-related Ayurvedic exercises, such as those that use colors to balance the doshas, can have the same effect. Your eyes are your windows on the world. Learning to use them well can benefit every aspect of your physical and spiritual health.

Eye MUDRAS

Mudra is an Ayurvedic term for a gesture that brings about a specific physical or spiritual effect. Most mudras are for the hands, but there are also exercises for the eyes that can stimulate particular areas of the brain. By making these eye mudras part of your daily routine, you can strengthen your intuition, your perceptions, and your ability to recall sensory experiences.

Visual Memory

- Looking up and to the left enhances memory of visual experiences. Move your eyes in this direction when you want to remember something you've seen.

Sound Memory

- Looking down and to the left, or horizontally to the left, strengthens your memory of sounds.

Physical Memory

- Looking down and to the right enhances your memory of physical activities and emotional experiences. Look in this direction to remember how you felt when you were performing a specific activity.

Greater Attention

- Looking up and to the right strengthens your response to visual stimulation. Practice this mudra in order to see with greater attention and awareness.

Sense of Hearing

- Looking horizontally and to the right helps develop sensitive hearing.

Sense of Smell

- Focusing your eyes toward the tip of your nose enhances your sense of smell.

Sense of Taste

- Looking down toward your tongue strengthens the sense of taste.

- Directing your eyes upward toward a point between your eyebrows strengthens your powers of intuition and insight.

YANTRAS

Just as a mantra can be used in meditation to quiet the mind and gain access to the silent space between thoughts, a visual expression called a *yantra* can also create a meditative state of restful alertness. A yantra is the visual representation of a mantra. The Sri Yantra in the program, for example, is the visual representation of the mantra *om.*

Meditation with the Sri Yantra

To begin, sit quietly and let your eyes rest on the yantra. Gaze comfortably, but with intention and awareness. Allow your mind to become silent—don't use a mantra or any other meditation technique as you gaze at the Sri Yantra pattern before you.

Let your eyes focus on the center of the pattern. The dot in the center is called the Bindu. It represents the unity that underlies all the diversity of the physical world.

Now let your eyes see the triangles that enclose the Bindu. The downward-pointing triangle represents feminine creative power, while the upward-facing triangle represents male energy.

Let your vision expand to include the circles outside the triangles. These represent the cycles of cosmic rhythms, and within each circle lies the notion that time has no beginning and no end. The farthest regions of space and the innermost particles of an atom both pulsate with the same rhythmic energy of creation. And it is present within you as well.

Notice the lotus petals outside the circle: They're pointing outward, as if opening. They illustrate the unfolding of our understanding, and the lotus also represents the heart, the seat of the self. When the heart opens, understanding comes.

The square at the outside of the yantra represents the world of form, the material world that our senses show us— the illusion of separateness, of well-defined edges and boundaries.

Finally, at the edge of the pattern are four T-shaped portals, or gateways. Notice that they point toward the interior of the yantra, the inner spaces of life. They represent our earthly passage from the external and material world to the realm of the inner and the sacred.

Take a moment to gaze at the yantra, letting the different shapes and patterns emerge naturally.

Now, soften the focus of your eyes. Your eyelids may droop a little, and your eyes may even seem to cross. Look at the dot in the center of the yantra, and then, without moving your eyes, gradually begin to expand your vision. Take in the edges of the screen or page, then the walls of the room.

Continue expanding your field of vision until you are taking in information from greater than 180 degrees. Notice how that information was there all along, though you just became aware of it.

Now reverse the process, refocusing back to the center of the yantra.

Gently close your eyes. Become aware of how much information we focus through our senses and how much is actually available to us. Can you still see the yantra in your mind's eye? Is your vision limited to what your two eyes can see? Or is it greater than that?

COLORS

Each of the three doshas is attuned to a particular kind of sensory experience. Vata is especially sensitive to sound, Kapha to smell and taste, and Pitta is very visually oriented. All the doshas, however, can benefit from color-based exercises to restore balance. Viewing colors that balance your mind body type is an effortless way to reduce stress and bring pleasure into your life.

Colors to Settle Vata

Vata, the air dosha, tends toward coarseness and dryness when unbalanced. This can be relieved by viewing the blue color of a natural body of water, especially the ocean. In general, Vata responds to colors that are warm, soft, and soothing, including gold, red, orange, yellow, or light shades of green or blue. Reduce colors that are very bright or very dark.

Colors to Settle Pitta

Pitta is associated with fire. When out of balance, it creates excessive heat in the body. The fire of Pitta can be cooled by viewing the dark green of a forest or an expanse of grass.

Cool and calming colors such as white, deep green, and deep blue are also helpful. Avoid yellow, red, orange, and any other really bright colors.

Colors to Settle Kapha

Kapha is the water dosha. It tends toward stillness, but can be stimulated by beautiful and dramatic displays of color. Viewing a sunrise or sunset can be highly beneficial to Kapha, which responds well to bright colors such as red, orange, yellow, and gold. Reduce colors such as white, green, and blue.

MASSAGE

Although we don't usually think of it as such, the skin is the body's largest organ—and it is also a rich source of healing substances. When stimulated by massage or another form of therapeutic touch, the skin produces antidepressants, hormones that enhance circulation, and powerful anticancer and antiaging substances.

The touch of a human hand on the body has immediate benefits for the emotions and the physiology, and Ayurveda has emphasized the importance of healing touch since ancient times. Every neurochemical found in the nervous system is also present in the skin, and since massage can help stimulate the production of these substances, it's especially effective for treating anxiety and other nervous conditions. Along with meditation, a healthy diet, and appropriate exercise, massage can be one of the foundations of continuing good health.

MARMA *Points*

According to Ayurveda, certain areas of the skin called *marma* points are junctions where mind and body meet. By stimulating the marma points with massage or yoga, you can bring healing effects to specific areas of the mind-body system.

- Stimulation of the forehead, between the eyes, promotes mental stability and clarity of thought.

- Stimulation of the throat stabilizes the powers of expression.

- Stimulation of the area over the heart stabilizes the emotions.

- Stimulation of the solar plexus, in the area of the diaphragm, stabilizes the body's center of gravity. The mind centers when the body is centered.

- Stimulation of the lower abdomen stabilizes sexual expression.

- Stimulation of the soles of the feet promotes sleep.

OIL MASSAGE
and the DOSHAS

Traditionally, Ayurvedic massage includes oils that provide specific benefits for Vata, Pitta, or Kapha. Both the type of massage that's best for you and the appropriate oil should be selected with an understanding of the needs of your mind body constitution.

Vata

Vata types, who tend toward worry and restlessness, can benefit from a gentle massage using oils such as sesame or almond, which are heavy and warm.

Pitta

Pitta types are prone to overheating and to heat-related conditions such as rashes and other irritations of the skin. Pittas should use a deep massage with cooling oils such as coconut and olive.

Kapha

Kapha types, who can become sedentary and sluggish when out of balance, respond best to vigorous, stimulating massage using a light oil such as sunflower or safflower. Dry massage, known as garshana, is also especially beneficial to Kaphas.

ABHYANGA

A daily oil massage stimulates the marma points, tones the body, and promotes the release of impurities. It keeps the muscles warm during the day and is especially beneficial for balancing Vata. This full-body oil massage, known as *abhyanga*, takes about ten minutes to perform.

Preparing the Oil

In preparing for your massage, it's best to select an oil based on the needs of your particular mind body constitution. Heavy, warm oils such as sesame and almond are best for Vata types; Pittas benefit most from cooling oils such as coconut or olive; and light oils such as sunflower or safflower are most appropriate for Kaphas.

Before use, cure your massage oil once by very slowly heating it in a glass or metal pot. Place a few drops of water in the oil as it heats. Then remove the pot from the stove as soon as the water boils out of the oil. Be sure to watch the oil carefully so that it doesn't burn.

Before performing the massage, the oil should be reheated above body temperature. To do this, put a small portion of oil in a plastic cup or squeeze bottle and place it in a bowl of hot water. Or it can be microwaved for ten to fifteen seconds.

Because some oil may spill, it's best to perform abhyanga in the bathroom. You may want to cover the floor with a large towel or plastic sheet.

Performing the Oil Massage

Begin by pouring a tablespoon of warm oil on your scalp. Massage your head with the flat of your hand, using circular motions, as if you were washing your hair, and then move to your face. Massage your forehead, and then move to your temples, using circular motions. Then rub around the ears.

Now apply a little oil to your hands. Massage the front and back of your neck using the flat of your hand and your fingers. Next, move to your shoulders. Massage your shoulders and then your arms, using circular motions at the joint areas and back-and-forth motions on the long parts.

Next move to your chest and gently massage, using circular motions. Then do the same to your stomach and lower abdomen.

Use up-and-down motions over your back and spine.

Then vigorously massage the legs, moving back and forth on the long parts and using circular motions on the knees and ankles.

Continue this vigorous massage onto your feet, using the flat of your hand except around the toes, which you can massage with your fingers.

As you complete the massage there should be a thin, almost undetectable, film of oil on your body.

Wash yourself with warm water and mild soap, leaving a bit of oil on your scalp if you want your hair to look glossy.

Performing the Mini Oil Massage

When there's not enough time for a full-body oil massage, you can perform an Ayurvedic minimassage in just one or two minutes. This minimassage focuses on the head and the feet, the parts of the body that will benefit most.

To begin the mini oil massage, pour a tablespoon of warm oil on your scalp. Massage your head with the flat of your hand as if you were washing your hair, and then move to your face. Massage your forehead, and then move to your temples, using circular motions. Then rub around the ears.

With a second tablespoon of oil, massage the feet vigorously, using the flat of your hand except around the toes, which you can massage with your fingers.

Sit quietly for a few moments to relax and soak in the oil. It is beneficial to leave a thin, almost undetectable, film of oil on your skin.

Dry MASSAGE

It is best to perform a dry massage, called *garshana* in Sanskrit, in the morning before bathing. It requires less than five minutes, and should be performed wearing special silk gloves, which are available from Ayurvedic sources. It is particularly good for pacifying Kapha imbalances. Since Kapha is an inherently oily dosha, dry massage is an excellent alternative to abhyanga. Garshana can also be used occasionally for Pitta, but it is generally not recommended for Vata, which is naturally a dry dosha.

Performing the Dry Massage

Begin by sitting on a stool or straight-backed chair. Then use both hands to massage your head in brisk circular motions. Shift to long strokes as you reach your neck and shoulders.

Use circular motions at the shoulder joints—long strokes on your upper arms—then circular motions again at the elbows.

Continue using long strokes down the lengths of your forearms, circular motions at the wrist, long strokes down the hands, and circular motions on the joints of your fingers.

Now move to your chest, and massage horizontally with long strokes. Dry massage should not be done over the breasts of women.

Now massage your stomach, using two horizontal strokes, followed by two diagonal strokes. Then alternate horizontal and diagonal strokes on the lower back, buttocks, and thighs. Give special attention to any area where extra fat is present, because massage can promote circulation and loosen toxins in these areas.

Now stand up and use circular motions to massage your hip joints. Then massage your legs, using long strokes over the long bones and circular strokes at the knees and ankles. Complete your massage with long strokes over your feet.

9

HERBS

For thousands of years humanity's primary healing substances came from naturally occurring botanical sources, and over the centuries Ayurveda has categorized more than twenty thousand herbs and herbal formulas. There are herbs for treating virtually any illness, as well as for the maintenance of overall good health.

Herbs are especially effective when they are used with an awareness of your individual needs and the nature of your mind-body constitution. They can be helpful in the early stages of doshic imbalance, and they can also support other treatments when illness is more advanced. But herbs are not "medicine" in the sense that the word has come to be understood. They are subtle forms of nutrition that can be used as supplements—not substitutes—for a well-balanced diet and appropriate health care. All the herbs discussed in this section can be taken either directly or as a tea. But, before using any herbs, be sure to discuss them with your health-care provider.

Herbal
CLASSIFICATIONS

Common Herbs

The following herbs are available in most grocery stores or health-food stores. You might even have them in your cupboard right now, or you may decide to grow them in your garden.

ALOE   (*Balances Vata, Pitta, Kapha*)

Aloe is often used externally on wounds and burns. Aloe's Sanskrit name—*kumari*—can be translated as "provides the energy of youth." Ayurveda recommends taking aloe as a juice to strengthen agni and to cleanse toxins from the blood.

BASIL   (*Balances Vata and Kapha*)

Basil is revered as a sacred plant in India, where it is believed to bestow faith, compassion, and the power of love. Basil is also said to clear the mind and strengthen memory. On the physical level, it alleviates cold symptoms by removing excess Kapha from the respiratory system.

BLACK PEPPER   (*Balances Kapha and Vata*)

Black pepper cleanses ama and is considered a powerful stimulant to digestion. Taken with honey, it is useful as an expectorant to relieve symptoms of respiratory infections and sinus congestion.

CAMPHOR (*Balances Kapha and Vata*)

Camphor clears the senses and sharpens perception. It can be applied externally as an oil, but Ayurveda also suggests taking small doses internally in the form of powdered crystals. As an incense, camphor is used by religions throughout the world to sanctify the atmosphere and facilitate meditation.

CAYENNE PEPPER (*Balances Kapha and Vata*)

Cayenne pepper stimulates digestion and circulation, burns away toxins, and counters the cold brought on by a Vata or Kapha imbalance. Because of its powerful heating effect, cayenne should be used sparingly, especially by individuals with Pitta imbalances.

CHAMOMILE (*Balances Kapha and Pitta*)

Chamomile is widely used as a tea to calm the nerves and promote sleep. It also benefits digestion and relieves headaches. Because of its mild action, chamomile is useful for stabilizing the system and balancing the effects of other herbs.

CINNAMON (*Balances Vata and Kapha*)

According to Ayurveda, cinnamon strengthens agni, the digestive fire, throughout the body and is particularly beneficial to the heart and kidneys. Like chamomile, cinnamon's mild effects make it widely useful. It does not aggravate Pitta and brings calm to unbalanced Vata constitutions.

GARLIC (*Balances Vata and Kapha*)

Garlic is one of the herbs most widely used throughout the world. It cleanses the circulatory and lymphatic systems, and has a healing effect on all areas of the system. Garlic has a generally calming effect, but long-term use is said to dull the mind.

GINGER *(Balances Vata and Kapha)*

Ginger is called a universal medicine by Ayurveda, and is considered one of the most sattvic spices. As a tea or chewed with salt or lemon, it stimulates the appetite, reduces ama, and relieves respiratory congestion. Dry ginger, which is hotter and more stimulating than fresh ginger, is useful for balancing Kapha and for strengthening digestion. Fresh ginger is best for pacifying Vata. It can also be used to treat colds and flu.

MINT *(Balances Pitta and Kapha)*

Peppermint and spearmint are mildly cooling herbs that relax the mind and facilitate thorough digestion. But not all mints are cooling. Thyme, for example, has a mildly heating effect, and is used for relieving intestinal gas.

NUTMEG *(Balances Vata and Kapha)*

Nutmeg helps digestion by stimulating absorption in the small intestine. Nutmeg also relaxes the nervous system and calms the mind, but if taken to excess it can bring on dullness and fatigue.

PARSLEY *(Balances Kapha and Vata)*

Parsley is an excellent nutritional supplement with a mildly warming effect on the system. It relieves premenstrual cramping and headaches, and alleviates water retention. Parsley is good for Kapha and Vata imbalances, but should be used moderately by Pitta types.

RASPBERRY (*Balances Pitta and Kapha*)

Raspberry cools Pitta, heals inflammations, and tones the muscles and skin. Its mildness makes it useful for relieving sore throats and diarrhea in children.

SANDALWOOD (*Balances Pitta and Vata*)

Sandalwood is often burned as an incense to facilitate meditation and devotion. It is said to open the third eye, and to promote spiritual awareness. Organically, sandalwood is a good anti-Pitta herb. It cools fevers and reduces inflammations.

SESAME SEEDS (*Balances Vata*)

Sesame seeds rejuvenate Vata but should be used sparingly by high Pitta constitutions because of their warming nature. Sesame seeds strengthen the tissues, especially the bones, and are useful in treating chronic coughs and digestive problems.

Cleansing Herbs

These herbs are useful for eliminating toxins from the physiology as a whole, or from particular areas of the system. They are available at many health-food stores or from the Ayurvedic sources listed in the Reference Section of the program.

AMALAKI (*Balances Pitta and Vata*)

Amalaki is considered the most important rejuvenative herb in Ayurveda. In Sanskrit, *amalaki* means "the sustainer," and it has benefits for a wide range of conditions. It restores tissues, cleanses the intestines, increases the red blood cell count, and is one of the best natural sources of vitamin C.

ASAFOETIDA (*Balances Vata and Kapha*)

Asafoetida is called *hing* in Sanskrit. An excellent cleanser of the digestive system, asafoetida can break up ama accumulations caused by unhealthy eating habits. It strengthens agni and dispels intestinal gas.

ECHINACEA (*Balances Pitta and Kapha*)

Echinacea has natural antibiotic properties and cleanses toxins from the body by energizing the lymphatic system.

GUGGUL (*Balances Kapha and Vata*)

Guggul cleanses and rejuvenates decayed tissue, increases the white blood cell count, and cleanses the skin and mucous membranes. It is especially effective for stabilizing Vata and Kapha imbalances without irritating Pitta. Guggul is the traditional Ayurvedic herb for healing arthritic disorders.

MANJISHTA (*Balances Pitta and Kapha*)

Ayurveda considers manjishta to be the most effective herbal blood purifier. It cleanses and balances the functions of many organs, including the liver, spleen, and kidneys. Manjishta helps heal injured or diseased tissue by increasing blood flow, and is useful as a first-aid remedy.

NEEM (*Balances Pitta and Kapha*)

Like manjishta, neem is a highly effective blood purifier and detoxifier. It's especially effective in treating chronic fevers and inflammatory skin conditions. When applied as a medicated oil, neem can also aid the healing of joint and muscle inflammations.

TAGARA *(Balances Vata and Kapha)*

Tagara is called valerian in English. It is especially effective for cleansing excess Vata from the blood and the digestive system. Tagara is also used to alleviate muscle pain and dispel menstrual cramps.

TRIPHALA *(Balances Kapha)*

A traditional Ayurvedic combination of three herbs (haritaki, amalaki, and bibhitaki), triphala is widely used in India as a bowel tonic. It is highly effective in removing stagnated ama from all areas of the digestive tract.

Healing Herbs

The following herbs can help in treating individual illnesses or infections concentrated in specific areas of the body. They are available at many health-food stores or from the Ayurvedic sources listed in the Reference Section of the program.

ALOE *(Balances Vata, Pitta, and Kapha)*

Aloe is known as *kumari* in Sanskrit. In many parts of the world it is used in first-aid treatment of wounds and burns, and is considered a potent blood cleanser. Aloe is also considered a rejuvenative for the liver and the female reproductive system.

AMALAKI *(Balances Pitta and Vata)*

Amalaki is traditionally recommended for healing blood, skin, liver, and bone imbalances. It has antibacterial and antiviral properties, increases red blood cell count, and is the best natural source of vitamin C.

ARDRAKA *(Balances Vata and Kapha)*

Ardraka is the Sanskrit term for ginger root, and is considered the "universal medicine" by Ayurveda. It strengthens the digestive fires without overheating the system and aggravating Pitta, and can also be used as an expectorant to cleanse the respiratory tract.

ARJUNA *(Balances Pitta)*

The classical Ayurvedic heart tonic, arjuna, is used to benefit both emotional and physical heart problems. In Sanskrit, *arjuna* means "open-hearted."

ASAFOETIDA *(Balances Vata and Kapha)*

Asafoetida, also known as hing, is a strong-smelling resin that cleanses the digestive system, stimulates healthy intestinal function, and dispels intestinal gas. It is especially effective in eliminating the toxic accumulations that develop from unhealthy eating habits.

ASHWAGANDHA *(Balances Vata and Kapha)*

A potent rejuvenative, ashwagandha is soothing to the neuromuscular system, and is useful in treating rheumatism and muscle pain. Ayurveda teaches that it also calms the mind. In English, ashwagandha is known as winter cherry.

BALA *(Balances Vata, Pitta, and Kapha)*

In Sanskrit, *bala* means "provider of strength and immunity." Ayurveda has traditionally used it to benefit rheumatism and urinary-tract infections. It has a strongly energizing effect on the system in general, and should be used cautiously by individuals with high blood pressure.

BRAHMI (*Balances Vata, Pitta, and Kapha*)

Through its cooling effect on Pitta, brahmi, also known as Indian pennywort, helps soothe nervous conditions such as anxiety and anger. It is also useful in treating chronic skin inflammations. In Sanskrit, *brahmi* means "that which expands awareness."

GOKSHURA (*Balances Vata, Pitta, and Kapha*)

Because it soothes the mucous membranes and lubricates the throat, gokshura is effective in healing chronic coughs and respiratory infections. Ayurveda teaches that it also calms the nervous system. It is known as caltrop in the United States, where it is often found growing in the wild.

GUDUCI (*Balances Vata, Pitta, and Kapha*)

The heating quality of guduci strengthens digestive fires and fosters the elimination of toxins from the system. It can also aid healing of skin disorders, rheumatism, and urinary-tract infections.

HARITAKI (*Balances Vata, Pitta, and Kapha*)

One of the most important Ayurvedic herbs, haritaki is especially beneficial in treating Vata imbalances. In Sanskrit, its name means "that which carries away disease." Haritaki is useful in a wide variety of conditions, including coughs, asthma, heart disease, jaundice, diarrhea, and hemorrhoids.

JATAMAMSI (*Balances Vata, Pitta, and Kapha*)

Jatamamsi, also known as musk root, has antibacterial and antifungal properties, and is also calming to the nervous system. It has reduced high blood pressure in animal studies and is considered by Ayurveda to be rejuvenative for the cardiovascular system.

KAPIKACCHU   *(Balances Vata)*

Kapikacchu, also known as cow-itch plant, is traditionally used to benefit nervous system and kidney disorders. It can also be useful for stabilizing weaknesses in the reproductive system.

LICORICE   *(Balances Vata and Pitta)*

Nourishing to all the tissues, licorice is particularly useful in treating the inflamed mucous membranes of colds and flu. The Sanskrit name, *yasht madhu*, means "honey stick."

NEEM   *(Balances Pitta and Kapha)*

Neem, which is sometimes known as Persian lilac, is effective in treating chronic fevers and inflammatory skin conditions. As a medicated oil, it can also be applied externally to heal joint and muscle inflammations.

SHANKHAPUSHPI   *(Balances Vata and Pitta)*

One of the most effective Ayurvedic nerve relaxants, shankhapushpi helps heal neuralgias and rheumatisms. It is often combined with brahmi to soothe anxiety.

SHATAVARI   *(Balances Pitta and Vata)*

Used as a rejuvenative for the female reproductive system, shatavari also calms gastrointestinal upset. The Sanskrit word means "able to have one hundred husbands." In English shatavari is known as Indian asparagus.

TULSI   *(Balances Vata and Kapha)*

Tulsi, also known as holy basil, is useful as an expectorant for respiratory congestion, and in the form of a tea for treating stomach pain. As a paste, it can be applied to the skin to soothe insect bites.

TURMERIC   *(Balances Kapha)*

Turmeric is known in Sanskrit as *haridra*, which means "to carry away illness." It is a natural antibiotic and blood cleanser, and helps alleviate the inflammatory effects of arthritis.

10

SOUND

Sound can soothe, and sound can strengthen. Your body can literally metabolize sound to produce healing chemicals, and music is especially valuable in this respect. When you hear a beautiful piece of music, every cell in your body responds to this experience, and the responses have a material form. They are molecules, just as all thoughts and feelings are molecules, and they are literally created by the music.

By understanding the transformation of sound into matter, you can gain insight into the essential mechanics of creation. And in your own life, you can learn to use this creative process to benefit body, mind, and spirit.

The
POWER *of* LANGUAGE

Language is an expression of sound's creative power, and it's easy to find examples of the profound effect that certain words can have on human consciousness. For example, in virtually all languages the word for *mother* begins with *m*. There seems to be a deep, preconscious association in the human mind between the *m* sound and the idea of nurturing or providing sustenance. Deep within human consciousness, this sound denotes the womb of creation. Ayurveda teaches that the images created by such a sound reside outside our physical selves. They exist in our subtle bodies, which will survive the death of our physical bodies, from which they originally came.

Primordial SOUND

Primordial sounds are the prelinguistic natural vibrations that form the structure of the universe. Once you learn to listen, you can hear these sounds throughout nature—in waves crashing against the seashore, in the wind blowing through trees, even in the songs of birds. Primordial sounds have been part of human experience for hundreds of thousands of years. They are literally structured into our DNA, and when we hear them our bodies instinctively synchronize with these ancient rhythms.

Listening to or repeating primordial sounds helps to quiet the mind and to stimulate the body's inner healing energy. In the form of mantras, these sounds are the basis of primordial sound meditation. *Om* is perhaps the best-known primordial sound mantra, but hundreds of mantras are described in Ayurvedic literature, each with a specific purpose and effect.

Since they're free of the associations that accompany everyday words, primordial sound mantras can interrupt the otherwise continuous train of thought that fills our minds at every moment. By silencing our internal dialogue and replacing it with one of the seed sounds of the universe, we can enter the gap between our thoughts and explore the silence that is the true foundation of our being.

Music to Balance the Doshas

VATA-BALANCING

Music to balance Vata has a calming, soothing quality. This can be achieved with various compositions ranging from Chopin's nocturnes to the sunset *ragas* of classical Indian music.

PITA-BALANCING

Pitta-balancing music has a relaxing and cooling effect, as found in medium-tempo Indian ragas or in the uplifting sounds of Pachalbel's Canon in D.

KAPHA-BALANCING

Music to balance Kapha is stimulating and energizing, such as Vivaldi's *The Four Seasons* or traditional Peruvian flute music.

As you begin to take some of the steps recommended in these pages and in the program, remember always to be easy on yourself. Some recommendations will work better than others or have a more immediate effect. If the number of suggestions seems overwhelming, just begin by adding the ones you can easily do, and keep reviewing the program so that, over time you can incorporate more.

The process of growth is ongoing. By gradually adding Ayurvedic elements to your daily routine, you'll find your life becoming increasingly harmonious and joyful. That's the ultimate purpose of everything you experience here: to help you restore simplicity to the mind body system, and to bring it back into accord with nature. My intention is to show you the way to total fulfillment, to let your life be guided by your truest self, to permeate every aspect of your being with the wisdom within.

For information on books, audiotapes, videotapes, and seminars by Deepak Chopra, please contact:

Infinite Possibilities Catalog
60 Union Avenue
Sudbury, MA 01776-2271
1-800-858-1808